D0283295

DRAMA FREE HOMEWORK

A PARENT'S GUIDE TO ELIMINATING HOMEWORK BATTLES AND RAISING FOCUSED KIDS

JOANN CROHN

Download the Audiobook for free

Thank you so much for buying my book! To show you how much I appreciate it, let me read it to you!

Download your free audiobook at:
noguiltmom.com/dramafreeaudio

Drama Free Homework: A Parent's Guide To Eliminating Homework Battles And Raising Focused Kids

DRAMA
FREE
HOMEWORK

PART 1:
The Problem of Homework

CHAPTER 1:

Is Independent Homework a Myth?

My daughter sat down at the kitchen table and cried. Her green homework folder rested next to her arm and the packet of Kindergarten homework lay in front of her. She flipped through the three pages of math, spelling and handwriting homework and slumped in her seat.

After six hours at school, sitting still and following directions, my girl was depleted.

I felt guilty.

As she was a December baby, we had the option of starting her in school a year early. This made sense. I was an early entry; my husband was an early entry and our daughter was tall, mature and already towered over other children, even though she was the youngest in class. I knew that starting her in Kinder as a four-year-old was the right decision.

Yet now the words of her preschool teacher echoed in my head. "Give her one more year to play," she advised.

Nope. My husband and I shook our heads. She's going to Kindergarten. She's ready. But now, as she sat before me at the kitchen table, eyes filled with tears, I wasn't so sure.

Did we do the right thing? Shouldn't she be coming home from school excited and ready for more?

My son was only three weeks old at the time, strapped to my chest in the hottest body swaddle known to man.

I scooted next to my daughter and tried to encourage her.

"Look, let's do one math problem at a time," I coaxed.

"NO!!! I can't do it! I don't want to!!" More tears.

Right now, this homework drama was the least of my

struggles. My son cried solidly from 4-7pm unless I rocked him or nursed him. He barely let me sleep at night.

My body ached; my head ached. I wanted to rip up my daughter's homework and throw it in our kitchen garbage. This is ridiculous! At that moment, I remember walking to our living room couch, sitting down and bursting into tears.

My daughter sat down next to me and whimpered.

I was a teacher at the time. Only one month into my maternity leave, I already wanted to claw my way back into the classroom. Teaching 30 ten-year-olds is *way* easier than being a stay-at-home mom,

Then I thought about my students. How would I get them to do work when they didn't want to? Hmmmmm... I had a lot of strategies to choose from.

I started trying the same things at home. Some worked for my daughter and some didn't, but within a month she and I both settled into a homework routine that was free of tears.

Now my daughter is a happy fifth grader who takes complete responsibility for her own homework and assignments.

Did I get lucky? I don't think so.

I used proven strategies to help my daughter develop her skills of focus, responsibility, time management, and persistence. These are executive functioning skills that every child can learn and improve on. I believe in this so fully that I created a course for kids called Homework 911 that teaches elementary school students how to set up their own homework routine and persevere.

The stories of families who've taken Homework 911 blow me away. I'll share them with you throughout this book as encouragement to know that there is a light for you, too. As a parent, you have a huge influence over your child's success.

Notice I said 'influence', not 'control'. Ultimately, your child's life is up to them but you can help shape it in little tiny ways. We teach our kids skills they can use to be successful later in life; how we react in moments of struggle can influence how they react when they encounter strife.

Defining 'Homework'

Yes, homework time can be annoying and frustrating, but as parents we're approaching this struggle completely wrong.

Instead of campaigning for no-homework policies, we can use homework to teach our kids valuable life skills, like:

- **_Prioritization:_** what should you do first
  and what can you completely half-ass? In
  our lives, we don't give our best effort to
  everything; we only have a limited supply of
  gumption to help us accomplish our personal
  goals. Therefore, we need to decide what is
  worth the effort and what isn't.
- **_Time Management:_** of all the stuff we need
  to accomplish, how can we do the stuff we
  hate in the least amount of time possible
  and make more time for the things which are
  important to us?
- **_Perseverance:_** how do we push through the
  assignments we hate or don't completely
  understand in order to experience success?
- **_Joy of Work:_** discovering the tasks we really
  love. Finding the work that makes us happy
  and enthusiastic is one of life's greatest gifts.

Our kids can learn all these skills through the practice
of homework... once we understand 'homework' in its
proper sense.

Before we get too far in, let me briefly say how
I define homework. There are multiple interpretations so
let's get this straight now:

Homework is work assigned to be completed outside of class that is either a practice of skills taught in class or an extension in a creative way. It is meant to be relatively quick, depending on the student's age, *and* **students should be able to do homework independently with little adult assistance.**

In other words, homework isn't your job.

Homework was never meant to be an extension of your work as a parent. Yet somehow we parents have developed the habit of sitting over our kids for every little assignment. I'm here to remind you this isn't helping you or your kids.

This book is meant to help you help your child become an Independent Homework Completer.

Whoa... that's a mouthful. But to put it simply, I'll help you learn to let go and help your child take charge of their own homework.

Why Should You Listen To Me?

I have my Masters in Elementary Education; I'm a National Board Certified Teacher; and I've spent six years in the elementary school classroom, teaching and helping students with differing abilities, home situations and attitudes towards learning.

During maternity leave with my son, I started the

website, *No Guilt Mom (www.noguiltmom.com)* to help parents feel less guilty about all things parenting. I do this by teaching strategies and research-based educational tactics for parenting as well as psychological self-care.

And I'm fun.

I will always be real with you. I'm not going to sugarcoat this process and say it's "so easy" or "super-simple". It's not.

But you can do it.

I'm going to walk you through this in an enjoyable way where we'll commiserate, laugh and hopefully not cry (however, crying is one of the best emotional releases *ever*, so if you need to use it, please go for it.)

So How Should We Approach Homework?

Our hearts beat faster and we feel a little lightheaded when our kid breaks down at the kitchen table and can't do his or her homework. We reassure them, "yes! Yes you can!" but then we look at the problem. Ummmm.... What exactly are they asking here? After multiple re-reads and attempts, we're stumped.

Most parents will be familiar with this situation, particularly in math with Common Core.

Or maybe your child fights you on your solution. For example, you see a relatively simple two-digit multiplication problem and think, "yes, I got this," but then your child jumps in to inform you that's not how his teacher told him to solve it.

"That's not the way Ms. Olson taught us to do it, Mom."

"Well, then how should we do it?'

"I don't knowwwwwwwww!" Then come the tears.

How many times has this happened to you?

Homework should be an independent activity, but if it's not that way for your family currently, don't worry. I'm going to get you there.

To give you hope, I want to share what happened with one of the families enrolled in my Homework 911 course. Ruth struggled to get her daughter, Annie, to do homework each night. Annie couldn't focus which usually meant hours of begging, pleading and yelling to get homework done. There were also a lot of tears - both from Ruth and Annie.

Now, Annie wasn't all that enthusiastic about taking a course on homework, but Ruth turned it on and it hooked her from the very first video. She watched the entire course in one sitting and then proceeded to do her homework WITHOUT BEING ASKED. Ruth said that has never happened! The best part? Annie has continued to do her homework without a fight since finishing the course.

Homework became an independent task for Annie

and that's what's going to happen for you, too!

The first thing to realize is, for homework to be independent, it should be a practice of skills kids have already learned in class. It should not be something new that you need to research and reteach. Here are three points we need to keep in mind as we begin this journey:

Point 1:

You'll need the teacher's support.

Teachers do make mistakes. I did when I was in the classroom. When I was a fairly new teacher with no school-age children of my own, our school subscribed to a program called MAC-RO.

MAC-RO had extremely good intentions. Every night, students were assigned five math problems covering grade-level concepts that represented what students would see on standardized tests.

However, many times the monthly booklet introduced concepts I had not yet covered in class. This created a ton of stress for families as parents scrambled to help their kids.

And some parents couldn't help at all.

As my students could not complete these problems

independently, I should have never assigned them as homework. If I could redo it, we would have done MAC-RO together as a class.

But no one called me on it. Yes, parents did express their concerns and say how long it took, but I missed their subtle hints. I was a naive 29-year-old who thought I knew everything about teaching because I had a degree.

Teachers are human and they make mistakes.

If you feel your child cannot complete his or her homework independently, that is not on you or your child. It is a subject that should be brought up with your child's teacher, clearly and directly.

Imagine you're talking to 29-year-old me, with my head completely in the clouds; you need to bring me back down to Earth. Tell me it's taking you hours to do homework, your child can't do it by his or herself and you need my help. Explain that all this homework packet has achieved has been fights and stress at home.

That should get me listening.

Point 2:

Kids should know how to motivate themselves.

We 're all forced to do unpleasant tasks (hello, pooper scoop in the backyard!) And yet, by the time we're adults, we know how to push through those less-than-desirable tasks to achieve the results we're after.

In fact, this is a necessary qualification to be successful. If success were all fun, everyone would get there.

Homework needs to be treated the same. Those twenty math facts need to be practiced. Those spelling words you don't know how to spell need to be written. That math worksheet you're scared of: the quicker you're into it, the quicker you're out.

As a parent, we don't have the time or energy to be a constant cheerleader to our kids. And, even if we did, it wouldn't serve them in the long run.

That's OK, because I'll teach you strategies that you can then teach your children on how to motivate themselves through difficult (and boring) assignments.

Point 3:

You need to help your kids manage their emotions.

As a very emotional person—I'm not exaggerating—
I've learned that often my own feelings pose the
biggest hurdle to getting things done. Simply sitting
down to write this book took a constant effort and
emotional joust. When I couldn't think of how to explain
a concept or became consumed with self-doubt,
I wanted to run to the fridge and bury my head in a large
bowl of ice cream (mmmmm, Ben & Jerry's Phish Food,
you're calling my name!).

Kids have this, too. The other day, my son flung
himself on the floor at the thought of writing all 15
spelling words. It was a new expectation. Ten was fine,
but fifteen... oh man, bring in the paramedics because
this is simply too much.

"I can't," he moaned, "I Can't... I CAN'T!"

Tantrums and outbursts happen whenever we're
overstimulated and overwhelmed. As adults, many of
us know how to rein in our emotions (or crush them
completely) and also use them to our advantage. Some
adults still use tantrums to get their way. You can
probably name a few people right now.

Our goal for homework and emotions is two-pronged.
We want our kids to:

- recognize their emotional limit and take a
  break; and

- see that controlled tantrums will not get them what they want.

Do you know a child who complains about writing a paragraph and, instead of starting the first sentence, collapses in a heap on the floor? It's exhausting being a parent. But don't fear, there is a way to stop this madness.

The Bottom Line: When Kids Work on Homework, You Should Be Able to Do Other Things

In fact, stepping in when your child is having a meltdown can actually make matters worse. When we're frustrated at not being able to help, it adds to the stress they already feel.

Research shows that, as a parent's confidence to help their kids with homework decreases, the level of stress in the home increases.[1] Conflicts over homework happen at least twice as often in homes where parents don't have at least a college degree. (With the new Common Core math, many parents with college degrees now experience the same stress!)

But this isn't how homework was intended to be. It isn't meant to be retaught; rather it's a practice of skills students have already learned and can, for the most part, complete independently.

If this isn't the case, it is not your fault nor is it your child's sole responsibility. Instead, it indicates that you need to schedule a time to talk with the teacher for further clarification, or a reduction or change in the homework assigned.

I know many parents hesitate talking with the school because they fear they themselves are doing something wrong.

That's where I'm going to help you. You should not need to sit beside your son or daughter during homework to ensure they complete their assignments. Together, we'll teach your child how to be confident in their homework routine, maintain focus and know when they need to ask you for help.

After that, if you're still seeing an inability to complete homework, you'll then feel confident approaching your child's teacher to ask for a change.

CHAPTER 2:

The Big Homework Debate

Recently, there's been an increase of news items about schools starting no-homework policies. A recent post by an Oklahoma teacher went viral because of a note she wrote home that read:

> *"Dear Parents,*
>
> *After much research this summer, I am trying something new. Homework will only consist of work that your child did not finish during the school day. There will be no formally assigned homework this year.*
>
> *Research has been unable to prove that homework improves student performance. Rather, I ask you do things that are proven to correlate with student success. Eat dinner as a family, read together, play outside and get your child to bed early."*[2]

"Yes!" parents say, "this teacher gets it." But are we missing something?

Is the problem really that homework is assigned or not assigned? Or is it the type or the amount of homework our kids are bringing home?

Work that your child doesn't complete in class and

brings home is still "homework' and can cause equal, if not more, frustration for parents. It's clear the issue isn't so black and white.

The History of Homework

If we look back in history, the homework debate has been cyclical. Starting in the early 1900s, teachers assigned homework because they felt it created more disciplined minds. But in the 1940s, families expressed growing concern that homework interfered with other home activities, so there was a fight to reduce it.

That was until the space race in the late '50s. When the Soviets launched Sputnik, many criticized the U.S. school system for lacking the necessary rigor to compete internationally. Therefore, homework increased.[3]

But by 1980, mental health professionals started to worry that the amount of homework was increasing students' stress, so the amount of homework fell until the passage of No Child Left Behind, a 2001 campaign that led to a complete focus on all students passing standardized achievement tests.

Truly, it's like watching a ping-pong match.

2001 marks when schools increased homework and started "teaching to the test". I did this as a fifth grade teacher in a high-poverty school where many families didn't even speak English at home. We knew poor test scores could affect the school's autonomy and all of our jobs, so we tried everything to prepare our students for that end-of-year test.

The pressure to perform was enormous. After my first year of teaching, I received a letter from the district office informing me that my students scored amongst the bottom 20 percent of all fifth graders in the district. Giving this kind of news to a first year teacher is deplorable, especially when it's not followed with any support. Not only that, it sends the message that a teacher's only goal is to get their students to pass a bubbled-in, multiple-choice test.

Did I mention over 60 percent of my students didn't speak English at home?

Everything in my class became geared towards preparing students for the all-important test every April. With only so many hours in a school day, the only way to increase students' practice and fluency of English was through homework.

The question is, was this the most appropriate use of their homework time? Homework needs to add to a child's learning and development. How this happens, according to Duke University researcher, Harris Cooper, who has studied the subject of homework for decades, depends primarily on the student's age.

In the early grades (K-3), homework should foster positive attitudes about learning, as well as relevant habits and character traits. It can also include a simple reinforcement of skills the student has already learned in class.

This can be reading a simple book, completing a page of basic math facts or even doing a family activity.

For kids in the upper elementary grades, homework should take a more direct role in improving student achievement: assignments like writing a paragraph, answering reading comprehension questions or practicing a math skill learned in class. In sixth grade and beyond, it should play an important role in improving standardized test scores and grades. Notice, though, this isn't until the sixth grade. The question is, since it has no impact on test scores until this point, does that mean homework is purposeless and should be dismissed?

Some think so.

Homework is Declining Again

Education policy is once again veering towards reducing homework. Many school districts across the U.S. are either banning homework, placing nightly time limits on homework or not allowing teachers to grade homework.[4]

With the current focus on student wellness, many of these measures make sense, particularly the nightly time limit. Less homework means more time for family activities, play and down-time. In today's high-achieving, college-admittance-obsessed world, kids need a break.

But refusing to grade homework altogether? Both teachers and parents are concerned.

Teachers use homework as a tool to finish classwork or to grade student proficiency. Imagine high school without writing a term paper at home.

Many parents aren't thrilled with the idea, either. Take Renee, a mom from Louisiana, whose children attend school in a district that banned the grading of homework for kids in the second through twelfth grade.

Renee has two kids. She never had to establish a homework routine with her oldest, who is now 21. She says she would come home from school, get her stuff done and was extremely responsible. Renee thought she had it all figured out.

Then her son came along and, says Renee, "totally blew it out of the water." He's functioning, but has very high anxiety. He has a tendency to get overwhelmed very easily, which makes it a struggle to get homework done.

She says he used to get off the bus, eat a quick bite at the kitchen table and then they would immediately start homework. The problem was, he would look at a page of

10 math problems and completely freak out. He thought he'd never be able to finish it.

So Renee would take that math sheet and do the first three problems with him. Then they would do a little bit of reading homework, which didn't overwhelm him as much. After reading, they would return to math. Starting in elementary school, she taught him how to break his homework assignments into manageable chunks.

She sees him take this same approach now in high school when he has to complete English papers. He does a little bit, takes a break and then comes back to it to prevent himself from getting overwhelmed. He learned this skill because he had homework in elementary school that he was accountable for.

Harris Cooper supports this claim. In a recent interview to the *Chicago Tribune*, he affirmed that while homework in the younger grades does not guarantee academic success, it does help students create study habits they can use in later grades.

Cooper says, "Is [homework] going to cause a great leap in [students'] achievement? No it is not. What it's really doing is shaping their behavior, so they begin to learn how to study at home."[5]

The new policy in her son's school district frustrates Renee. Now her son is no longer responsible to the teacher, he doesn't do his homework. She's scared as to how this is preparing him for life after high school. Now, she looks up the assignments he hasn't finished in class and makes him sit down and do them.

As a parent, Renee saw the benefits of homework and she's not alone. Without homework, many parents aren't aware what their kids are doing in the classroom and parent-school communication falls apart. Also, since math benefits from daily practice, schools with no homework have seen their math scores decrease.

Overall, the research backs up the benefits of nightly homework. One research analysis showed that an average student in the tenth to twelfth grade age range who had appropriate homework assigned, scored 23 percentile points higher than a student with no homework.[6]

In grades 4-6, the gain was six percentile points. Small, but still present.

Note the magic word here is "appropriate". Not mindless busywork, nor homework where kids can't seem to get off the struggle bus; but home assignments kids can do independently, that still pose a small challenge and develop the skills that benefit from practice.

CHAPTER 3:

What is 'Appropriate Homework'?

O h, spelling! How do you teach spelling as a teacher? Frankly, I didn't know.

Growing up, I had always been a good speller. I thought it was due to the way I devoured *The BabySitters Club* books under my desk when my fourth grade teacher was teaching; or how I would stay up late reading some cheesy young adult mystery—usually involving shrunken heads and ancient Mayan tombs.

What I didn't realize was that I was a phonetic speller. I could split apart the words in my head into the separate syllables and spell each individually. No one taught me how to do this, but after so much reading I did it automatically.

So much so that I pronounced the word "whodunit" as WOD-UNIT for the longest time!

In my beginning years as a teacher, possibly because spelling came so naturally to me, I didn't know how to teach spelling to my students. There was a large, gaping chasm between those who had mastered their phonics skills and the kids who saw spelling as an impossible memorization task.

So, as a fifth grade team, not knowing any better, we decided it would be best to drill the weekly spelling list into them. My colleague and I created this monster spelling packet where kids needed to alphabetize all 20 spelling words, then break them apart into syllables, then write sentences using each word.

I'm fairly certain that our homework packet appeared in many of our students' nightmares. We thought that, by being tough, we would get results.

What happened? Most of our students didn't do the work. Some did, but those were the ones who always did the work. The kids who could take a spelling list and ace the Friday test with no further instruction from me.

However, the other 80 percent of the class, the ones we wanted to help improve, didn't.

We took away recess.

We excluded them from fun activities.

They eventually completed their packets.

I bet they hated it. And it didn't change their weekly spelling test score one bit. But, thinking any homework was better than nothing, I continued assigning the dreaded spelling packet.

It wasn't until one of our curriculum coaches pulled us aside and asked, "How would you feel if you had this homework?" that I seriously considered the effect the packet had on students. How would I feel? Well... not happy. I'd probably make up funny names for the teacher and talk about her behind her back.

Finally, I understood: this homework was not 'appropriate'.

Homework Problems Don't Always Stem from Your Child

In my determination to help my students improve their spelling, I had lost sight of what it means to set good homework that reinforces learning or expands creatively on what we covered in class.

This spelling packet was not appropriate homework because:

- it was not challenging—just busy work.
- it was unreasonably long.
- writing spelling words multiple times has absolutely *no effect* on your ability to spell the word.

As parents, if you can recognize inappropriate homework, you can identify whether homework issues actually stem from your child, or whether a conversation with the teacher is in order.

In general, teachers want to support their students. I'm happy my curriculum coach stepped in when she did!

Another way to judge whether homework is appropriate is to look at the amount of parental involvement it requires. While our spelling packet didn't require much parental input, many assignments do. In some cases, parents need to reteach major concepts to kids.

Nicole, a mom from Massachusetts, found herself doing this when her daughter was in the fourth grade. It wasn't the best circumstance: her daughter unfortunately had a teacher who was unwilling to talk to parents, believing instead that the kids should advocate for themselves.

I get the logic behind that policy, however nine-year-olds still need a bit of parental help when talking to authority figures. Her fourth grader was struggling in math, so Nicole looked up lessons on YouTube that taught her the Common Core Math subjects, which she would then re-teach to her daughter.

Nicole did what she needed to do as a parent. However, I argue that her daughter should have never been sent home with homework she couldn't do independently. Situations like this do not benefit the child or the family. Homework not only becomes frustrating for the kid but it becomes a source of parental stress as well.

Educational researcher, Robert Marzano, suggests that teachers should instead involve parents in appropriate ways. For instance, acting as a sounding board for a key concept. However, **parents should not be expected to reteach or police students' homework completion.**

That's not your job. If you find you are doing that, it is worthwhile to talk to the teacher.

How Much Time Should Kids Spend on Homework?

The national PTA association suggests that students receive 10-20 minutes for first grade and then 10 minutes per night for each grade thereafter. In the elementary grade levels, homework is not meant to improve standardized test scores. Rather, its purpose is to develop study skills and keep parents informed of what is going on in the classroom.

Every elementary school has a homework policy, which you can usually find online or in the student rules and procedures manual that most schools distribute at the beginning of the year.

The schools I've worked at, and those my kids have attended, follow the homework guidelines of the PTA pretty closely. When I taught, I tried to assign 30 minutes of math homework per night, followed by 20 minutes reading a book of the student's choosing.

The PTA guideline exists because the amount of homework needs to be appropriate for the student's age. When a young student has too much homework, it can cause problems.

A friend of mine told me that homework with her first grader took an hour and a half every night. After spelling, reading and math, her family had very little time for activities other than homework. My friend hated her evenings and dreaded opening her daughter's backpack. Instead of relaxing after a long day, she spent her nights sitting by her daughter at the kitchen table, cheering and persuading her. No one had any fun.

Worse yet, her daughter's attitude towards school dropped. She started to dread schoolwork.

If this is happening in your home, the suggestions in the following chapters are going to fix the problem. But, if you try them and they still haven't decreased homework to the recommended amount, it's time to bring it up with the teacher.

Remember me assigning the spelling packet from hell? No one is perfect (not even teachers!) If your family is struggling, other parents are struggling too.

CHAPTER 4:

Parent Dramas

My goal is to take the drama out of homework for your family. This involves teaching your kids new behaviors and helping them manage their emotions when things get hard. However, as parents we also need to do a quick check-in on our own emotions to be sure we're not getting in the way.

How parents personally feel about homework influences how their children feel about the whole homework experience. Research backs this up: a 2011 study of parents of fourth graders found that when parents demonstrated a positive attitude toward homework, their children felt more motivated to complete their assignments.[7]

This is logical. If we don't feel homework is worthwhile, have bad homework memories from our own experience or experience a traumatic situation relating to our kids and school, it's unlikely we'll manage the homework situation to the best of our ability.

When we parents have our own 'homework dramas', we're more likely to give in to the child's behavior, over-police our kids or even do their homework for them.

And that rarely gets us the results we want.

Here are a few questions to ask yourself before you look at your child:

Question 1:

Do you think an assignment is worthwhile?

If your child has been bringing home a lot of busy work or you feel that Common Core Math is ridiculous, you might have a negative attitude toward your child's assignments.

That's OK.

If you can't see the worthiness of an assignment,

question it. Send an email to your child's teacher. Ask for input from other parents in your child's class to explain what skill kids are supposed to learn. Perhaps the directions are unclear.

Do this in a kind way, of course. Seek understanding instead of desiring to prove the teacher and school wrong. Once you get clarification on the reasons behind an assignment, you'll be more likely to display a positive attitude towards the work, which will improve your motivation to help your child complete it.

Question 2:

What was your experience of homework at school?

We all carry around scars from elementary school. When I started my master's program in education, my professor polled the class:

"How many of you feel you aren't good at math?"

Half the class raised their hands.

Why? Because they had told themselves they were never "math people". Even more disturbing is that this belief has become an acceptable phobia. Students admitted it freely to their professor—the woman in charge of their grades—the first day of class.

Let me break it to you: There's no such thing as a "math person".

If you have this belief, I guarantee it will carry over to your child and impact how she views math as well.

The same goes for writing. Do you remember struggling to write that five-paragraph essay? Maybe your pencil hovered over the paper and a knot tightened in your stomach because you couldn't think of anything to write. Then, when your teacher returned it to you, you found she marked it up with red pen.

Or reading. Maybe you always struggled with those comprehension questions. You couldn't figure out what they were asking, nor where to find it in the text. Thus, you deemed reading comprehension to be a total waste of time.

These experiences still affect you as an adult. If you find yourself becoming unreasonably frustrated with your child's homework, look back to your past because something there is often to blame.

Question 3:

Is a new method freaking you out?

Let's talk Common Core.

I always tell parents that Common Core gets a bad rap. It's one of those subjects that would benefit from a great public relations campaign. However, since it's government-funded, that's not going to happen so let me do my best to finally give Common Core the good PR it needs.

These standards are a completely different approach to math. Notice I said 'different', not 'stupid' or 'unreasonable'. There are some very good reasons for this new approach. The math we learned in elementary school asked us to memorize formulas and perfect a specific system to solve a problem. As a result, math didn't make sense to a large percentage of students.

Do you remember the rhyme when dividing fractions?

"Yours is not to question why, just invert and multiply."

That is what was wrong with the way we were taught math! We weren't taught to question or understand exactly why we were doing something. Our teachers simply expected us to memorize a procedure—referred to as an algorithm—and replicate it.

Like a monkey.

Common Core takes a different approach. Instead of teaching one approach to solving a problem, it teaches kids multiple ways. Ways that conceptually make sense.

But, here's the issue:

Because of the way Common Core was rolled out, and the nature of standardized testing at the end of each year, schools are applying the old way of teaching math to the new Common Core approach.

For example, there are many ways to teach two-digit multiplication now, one of which is the area model which asks kids to visually draw the multiplication problem. It's super-cool and helps students see exactly how multiplication works.

However, teachers are taking this *one* way to solve it and making students repeat it over and over again. This isn't teaching for understanding; it's teaching the exact same way as the old math.

Expecting students to do things like a monkey.

When parents see a way to solve a problem that they're not familiar with, the natural instinct is to freak out. But remember, you do not need to reteach your child. If the process doesn't make sense to the student, they are not yet independent enough to have that assignment as homework.

Talk to the teacher. Other kids are probably having the exact same issue and the teacher can address it by devoting more time to that particular method or by teaching your child another method that makes more sense to her.

Question 4:

Do you hate the skill your child has to learn?

How did you feel about writing in school?

Me? I hated it. I remember bringing home my weekly book report assignment in fourth grade and then sitting at our kitchen table for hours. Each sentence was a struggle.

Seeing our kids go through this same struggle makes many of us parents want to quit and let them off the hook. Or we go in the other direction.

We push them through a tortuous experience, police their work and raise our own stress level in the process, thinking it's for their own good.

It isn't. By doing this, we're implicitly teaching that homework is not their responsibility. Instead, they learn that someone will always make them do their homework and motivate them through it.

We have to let our kids struggle. My parents did the right thing by leaving me alone to finish my book report every Sunday afternoon. They didn't interfere or persuade me to write. Even though I struggled with writing for many years, I eventually grew to appreciate it.

Look now. You're reading my book.

Question 5:

Do you have scars from a traumatic experience?

Kate's eight-year-old son cried through every minute of his homework. The tears started before he took his pencil out and placed his homework on the table. She felt his reaction was due to him working so hard throughout the school day and then being overwhelmed when he came home.

But it went deeper than that.

At the end of second grade, her son started to become physically sick at the mere thought of going to school. He threw up; he complained of headaches so Kate had to keep him home... a lot. Over the summer, the symptoms completely vanished. Then, when he started third grade, it all came back.

Even though he is doing better now, that period scarred Kate. She doesn't want to push her son through homework because of what they both endured less than a year ago.

Unpredictable situations like these are incredibly scary. Kate reached out for help from a local business that is now helping her son manage his stress. It's taking time but she's seeing little improvements in his attitude already.

However, this experience will probably forever impact the way she approaches homework. Scars like these, from either a traumatic event or our own school background, inevitably affect how we parent.

So how do we minimize the impact of these scars? First, be aware they exist.

If you feel that a past situation may be clouding your judgment, naming that fear is the most important step to conquering it.

I can't speak to a situation where this has happened to me with homework, but I can tell you a story about my dogs (dogs are our children, too, right?) One Saturday night, I played with my older dog, Lily, in our upstairs hallway. We had this game where we'd lunge at each other. She would start barking at me, then I'd chase her down. It was a fun time.

We don't play it anymore.

That Saturday night, our one-year-old rescue mutt, Addy, came trotting down the hallway and, thinking she was protecting me, attacked Lily. Addy's jaws chomped into the fold under Lily's ear and would not let go. I straddled the two dogs, trying to pry Addy's jaws open while Lily whimpered in pain.

We did finally get Addy off. Lily had a one-inch gash under her ear but after a few stitches, she's totally fine.

I, on the other hand, was not fine. I walked in fear around our house for months. I pictured the attack over and over again. I wouldn't let Lily come near me for fear that Addy would attack her.

Therapy helped me see that I was scarred by the attack. Once I realized that, I took the second step toward minimizing its effect: I became proactive in my discipline of Addy. Instead of shyly turning to the side when she jumped on me, I thrust my knee out with a loud, "*No!*". Instead of not petting Lily around Addy, I demanded Addy leave whenever Lily wanted my attention.

The dog attack made me stronger, just like your own traumatic event will make you tougher—as long as you name it and then take proactive steps to regain control.

The good news? You're reading this book. That says to me you're already being proactive.

We're Not Looking for Perfect Here

Your opinion of homework and past experiences will directly impact the way you react to your child as she struggles through her assignments or complains how something might be "too hard." You may empathize, or you may get mad at the homework and mad at the teacher.

However, a word of warning...

One thing I know we all do as parents is think we should do better. Most moms are quick to blame themselves if something goes wrong. The last thing I want to do with this chapter is give you another reason to blame yourself for your child having a difficult time. What I do want is for you to see another way you can make homework time just that little bit easier for you and your kid.

Knowledge is power. By taking your own dramas off the table, you will quickly see dramatic results with your child.

So next time you find yourself getting frustrated, stop. Take a step back and ask yourself these five questions to get to the root of your anger.

Again, they are:

#1 Do you think an assignment is worthwhile?
#2 What was your experience with school?
#3 Is a new method freaking you out?
#4 Do you hate the skill your child has to learn?
#5 Do you have scars from a traumatic homework experience?

It may not be the assignment, but rather that a past experience is clouding your interpretation of it.

Children are the best mirrors. Once your child sees your reaction, they, too, will have the same response towards the work. This is why stopping and regrouping is key. Once you're able to show a positive attitude toward homework time, you'll find your child will change her outlook as well.

CHAPTER 5:

Is This Your Child?

During my research for this book, I talked to many parents of elementary school students. Some were struggling with a homework routine and some were excelling. I wanted to know exactly how parents were supporting their kids and working through challenges.

One major trend I noticed is that moms are way too hard on themselves.

Most women told me how they hated homework

time because their kid cried and resisted. They felt like they were personally failing as parents and were totally unequipped for this.

After talking to them more and hearing what they were doing, I realized these moms were assessing their actions too harshly. They had strategies in place and were incredibly responsive to their children's needs. However, since their child was still struggling, many felt like failures.

If you feel like you're struggling with homework, you're probably in a similar space.

The women I talked to searched for method after method to help their kid succeed. They were simply stuck in the messy middle—that uncomfortable place where you haven't yet found an acceptable solution and are still searching in the dark with your flashlight beam darting around.

Struggle does not mean you're a horrible parent; it means your child is resisting a change. That's completely OK.

As these parents described their kids' homework-time behaviors to me, I saw four personalities appear over and over again:

- The Quick Quitter
- The Perfectionist
- The Emotionally Overloaded Kid

- The Oblivious Dreamer

You may read these and be able to identify two or three in your child; that's fine. Let's break these down; and with each I'll suggest specific tactics you can use.

The Quick Quitter

> "Homework that students cannot do without help is not good homework and is de-motivating. Homework should make students feel smarter, not dumber."
>
> – Cathy Vatterot

We've talked about appropriate homework already: homework that kids can do independently but which still provides a moderate amount of challenge. If the homework seems like it falls within these bounds but you're still having trouble, then something else is going on.

It may be that your child is throwing a tantrum or playing dumb to get out of the actual work. They may not believe they are "smart enough" to handle the challenge; or possibly the cries and tantrums of the past have gotten them out of doing the work.

I'm guilty of this as a mom. In fact, in our house

I was known for a while as the "yes" parent. When my kids asked my husband to do something and he was concentrating on his own work, his gut response was always to say "no".

He's pretty consistent on this, so our kids learned to stop asking him when he was busy.

Me, on the other hand... Somehow, my brain figured out that the quickest way to get my kids to stop asking me questions and let me concentrate—whether it be responding to email, writing or reading—was to say, "yes".

Of course, this works in the moment because they immediately stop bothering me, but oh... the repercussions!

By the way, I would do this totally unaware of what I was agreeing to. Later on that day, when my daughter called her friend to come over, or I found both of them using the couch to do somersaults, they always said, "But you said yes."

Oh, crap.

I've done the same with the "I don't knows" of homework.

I wanted them to be done in the shortest time possible, so I let the answer slip—just so my child could move onto the next problem. When I realized I was doing this, I physically restrained myself from helping. If I thought my daughter gave up too easily, quitting a math problem without thinking through any of the clues on the page, I found a way to leave the room.

"Oh no, I forgot a terribly important item upstairs. I'll be back. You keep working."

If you're dealing with a child who gives up before she even begins to try, you can:

- help her find the facts in the problem that will help her solve it.
- have him read the problem aloud to you.
- skip the problem and have your child write a note to the teacher that she didn't know how to do it.

That last step is far underutilized by parents. Kids usually have a healthy fear of their teachers and don't want to disappoint them. I find that asking the kids to admit to a misunderstanding that's not even true, will provide the necessary motivation to try it themselves.

The Perfectionist

How OK is your child with mistakes? Does she accept them? Or do you anticipate a full-out nuclear meltdown if something goes wrong?

Everybody makes mistakes. But not everyone handles them in the same way.

I'm the mother of two recovering perfectionists. Yes, they're young, but with a lot of work and reassurance they're not quite as hard on themselves as they were when they first started school.

I remember my daughter trying to read one of those take-home readers at the beginning of first grade. She was making way too many mistakes for her liking. I thought it was normal.

She threw the book down on the kitchen table, ran to our living room couch and just bawled:

"I'm never going to be able to read!!"

"Yes, you will sweetie. It just takes a ton of practice and making lots of mistakes"

"*Nooooooo*!!!!" Not mistakes!

Having perfectionist kids is killer, especially if you tend to be a perfectionist yourself.

I am.

But it's good to realize this, step back and see how your behavior looks to the outside world. I saw my daughter collapse on the couch and I thought, "Yep, I think I had that reaction to the National Board Certification process as a teacher."

Perfectionists view mistakes as the devil. Every time they misstep, they blame themselves.

Why couldn't I get that right?

This is never going to work.

I'm just not smart enough...

Left unchecked, this is the narrative that goes through the perfectionist brain. Thankfully, there is information we can share with our kids that will help them through this thought process until they develop a different attitude to their work.

Teach about Mindset

According to Stanford psychologist, Carol Dweck, there are two types of mindsets in the world: the fixed mindset and the growth mindset.[8]

Fixed mindset is what our perfectionist children—and many times we ourselves—struggle with. This mindset believes you are born as smart as you'll ever be: some people have the gift and some don't.

This is not saying that fixed mindset people believe they're dumb; they don't. In fact, they can believe they're incredibly intelligent. However, when a challenge comes along that they don't know how to solve, they quit. The challenge is stupid, of course. It's not them. They're smart, so this thing must be impossible and unworthy of their time.

Fixed mindset people can also take the attitude that when something is hard, they won't even try. The way they see it, they won't ever get it.

I get that way of thinking; it's how I operated through middle school and high school. Even today, I find that I give up on things before I even try.

But simply knowing that's my tendency helps me overcome it. When things get a little too hard in my business, the knowledge of my fixed mindset keeps me going and I push through rather than quit. This is why we need to teach our kids about it.

Allow me to debunk another theory that fixed mindset people hold onto: IQ. Popular belief is that IQ can tell how smart a person is. For a fixed mindset individual, this isn't helpful: I never took an IQ test because I was afraid of failing it. But did you know IQ was never meant to measure someone's set intelligence? Instead, it was created by a French psychologist to—get this—measure the impact of the French school system.

I.Q. measured how well a student's *environment* helped him or her learn. If a student showed a low I.Q. score, school administrators took that as a sign to move the student to a different program. Alexander Den Heijer once said, "When a flower doesn't bloom, you fix the environment in which it grows, not the flower."

That's I.Q. It identifies opportunities to *grow* the mind, not fix it in stone.

This leads us to the growth mindset, which acknowledges that the mind can grow and change.

A person with a growth mindset views the mind as a muscle: the more the muscle is worked, the stronger it gets. It's similar to going to the gym.

The first time you go, you pick up a five-pound weight and do some bicep curls. At the end of three sets of 10, you feel sore and tired. But then you rest and do it again. And again. Pretty soon, you progress to an eight-pound weight.

To a person with a growth mindset, the mind works the same way. The more you stress it appropriately, the more it grows.

Kids who know about the growth mindset—or possess it naturally—are more likely to persist towards their goals. They are the ones who encounter a challenge and, instead of quitting, work harder.

If your child doesn't have the growth mindset, its OK. Studies show that simply teaching them about the growth mindset helps them develop it. Carol Dweck and her team led a series of mindset workshops for adolescents where they taught about the brain and how one can grow it.

Teachers of the students in the workshops—who, by the way, did not know what the workshops entailed—reported that they saw real changes in the motivation of their students to learn and improve. Here's one of the comments:

"M. was far below grade level. During the past several weeks, she has voluntarily asked for extra help from me during her lunch period in order to improve her test-taking performance. Her grades drastically improved—from failing, to an 84 on her most recent exam."

How do you take your child from a fixed mindset to a growth mindset? Start talking to them about a major struggle that you went through. One where you waded through disappointment and ultimately felt it would be easier to just give up.

The story I tell my daughter is of my National Board Certification as a teacher. It was an intense process where I had to write four 15-page papers proving how I helped students learn. As detailed as a court brief, I had to provide examples of student work, along with their before and after scores. The National Board also required me to film myself teaching two lessons I created, then analyze each video to prove I was an accomplished teacher.

In addition to this, I sat for a three-hour written test covering six subjects in depth. To make matters worse, all my work was due in March and I wouldn't find out if I passed until November.

You need 275 points to achieve National Board Certification status. My first year through, I received 255. I was crushed. Heartbroken. I think I cried off and on for about a month whenever I thought about it. But then I pulled myself up, chose two papers to redo and submitted again.

The night of score release, I madly refreshed my computer while sitting on our living room couch... 274.

Are you kidding me? *One point off*!! Another year of waiting for one measly point? But this time I had no doubt I could do it. I could achieve that one point. One year later—three years after I started the process—I finally nailed it with a score of 283.

That agony of waiting and failing, waiting and failing again until my final victory taught me that mindset is everything.

Find your story of failure and perseverance and share that with your kids. If you can't think of one, take that dream you've always wanted and go for it with everything you have. You'll show your kids the power of mindset and how the upset of struggle can eventually become the sweetest reward.

The Overwhelmed Child

When I don't want to do something—like, *really* don't want to do something—I get emotional. You may do it, too. If you ever want to cry just thinking about doing all the dishes piling up in the sink, this will speak to you.

We're stressed. We're overwhelmed. It's a natural

reaction and some people are better handling it than others.

Our kids get this way, too. After all the after-school activities and demands on their time, kids get understandably tired.

Kendra, a mom from Chandler, Arizona, says this is exactly how her son reacts to homework. She explains that, "if he's mad and tired, he's writing mad and tired."

When our kids cry and look miserable, it triggers a huge protective instinct in us parents. We hate seeing them this way and think of any way we can make it better. Sometimes that means giving in and releasing them from homework for the night; or maybe it means you're by their side as their personal cheerleader - cheering them through math, one painful equation at a time.

"C'mon you can do it. Just one more. Just one more."

I release you from that responsibility. Not only does it stress you out, but your kiddo can feel your stress as well.

Instead, once you notice the emotional swell approaching, give your kid an active break. Family psychologist, Dr. Lisa Bravo, advises that some kids just need to move and run. Therefore, it's best to give kids a bit of unstructured time and let them move their bodies in any way they wish when they get home.

If your kiddo is way too emotional to start homework as soon as they get home, it is perfectly OK to delay until they're ready. Homework does not need to be done first thing if it doesn't benefit the child.

In addition to waiting until your kid is emotionally ready, you can also make the homework less overwhelming by breaking it into chunks. This is not to say that you have to supervise every chunk. Showing your kid how to focus on a little bit at a time is a great productivity skill.

You may remember the story of Renee and her son. As an elementary school student, her son hated sitting down to do math assignments. He fought her and resisted. So, she taught him how to break every assignment into manageable chunks of 3-5 problems at a time. He would finish those three problems, then do something else, come back and do the next chunk of problems and then eat dinner. This process continued until he finished the assignment.

Now, he's in high school and still using the strategy with other assignments, like essays for English class. The chunking strategy helped Renee's son complete his homework as well as keep his stress level low. We'll go over this strategy more in Part 2, when we talk about using a timer and other methods to make homework seem easier.

Irene, a Homework 911 aunt and her second grade niece Maya, used another tactic to keep emotions under control. Maya decided **how** she would do her homework in addition to when and where. For her, that meant rocking out the Hamilton soundtrack.

Irene explains there is now less drama and more pride in her niece during homework time because of the new control she feels. Homework has become "sorta fun."

Become a Tantrum Detective

But what if your child's emotions boil into a full-blown tantrum? Then, you need to step back and consider what kind of tantrum it is.

Is it a tantrum because his brain has become completely overwhelmed and can't function anymore? Or is it a tantrum to manipulate? How can you tell?

With a simple little test.

First, try to calm the child. Hold them. Tell them why you think they're upset.

For instance, "I know you're tired. You don't want to do homework right now. You thinks its too hard." Your child will do one of two things:

- They will either agree with you: you got it right. That's exactly why they're upset; or
- they will correct you and tell you the real reason they're crying.

With that info, you can remedy the situation. If they're tired, you can suggest a break or a snack to cool down before they start working again.

If they feel it's too hard, ask them to pick the problems or assignments they can do easily first. Once they get started with the easy stuff, 90 percent of the time they'll continue working. It's getting started that's the hard part.

Once your child is working calmly, ask yourself this critical question:

"What did she get out of her tantrum?"

Did she get your full attention? Did she get you to do some of the problems for her?

Remember, don't blame yourself for any of this. You're just gathering information. Think of yourself as a journalist collecting data to determine the cause of some salacious news story. Asking these questions helps you pinpoint the reason the tantrums occur. Once you know the cause, you'll probably find you're able to resolve the tantrums easily.

Take Sandra, for instance.

Her ten-year-old, Jeremy, always broke down in tears when she asked him to start his homework each night. She thought she understood why: his schedule was extremely packed. After school, she picked him up and drove him to baseball practice for an hour. Jeremy came home hungry and not in the mood to do homework.

There was no help for their schedule—he loved baseball—so homework would just be a necessary evil they needed to slog through. After months of this, she accepted his behavior as "normal' until she paid attention to Jeremy's emotional breakdowns—specifically, the moment he stopped crying and started working.

It happened the moment she or her husband, Ryan, stepped in to guide Jeremy through his homework, often doing the thinking for him and telling him to write down what they said.

She hated that her son had fallen into this habit of learned helplessness. It wasn't helping him learn or develop confidence in his abilities.

She knew he was tired and that he really enjoyed spending time with her and her husband. So, when they arrived home, she waited on homework. Instead, she let Jeremy have some down time. She didn't structure it.

Then she asked him when he wanted to do his homework. Jeremy decided he wanted to play a bit on his tablet when he came home and start his homework after dinner.

By giving Jeremy control over when he did his homework, as well as a bit of rest time, Sandra saw an immediate improvement in how he handled his assignments. He regained control of his emotions because now it was his choice to work on it and his parents became consultants on his homework instead of enforcers.

Sandra's still trying to break Jeremy's habit of milking his parents for answers, but she's seeing steady improvement.

The Oblivious Dreamer

Perhaps your child doesn't get stressed by homework. In fact, she doesn't seem stressed by anything. Sounds good, but there's a downside. Deadlines have no effect on her. Goals? She could really care less. She likes to have fun and live in the moment.

When I'm wound like a giant spring ready to snap, I find myself jealous of this personality. There are tons of benefits to having a carefree nature—these personalities have more fun for one thing. And rest assured, as much as their lackadaisical attitude frustrates you now, your child will eventually find her groove.

Right now, however, it's a daily struggle because:

- the threat of missing assignments means nothing to your kid; and
- they don't really care if they disappoint anyone regarding schoolwork.

Since nothing you enforce motivates them, it's worth giving your dreamer choices about the how, when, and where of doing homework.

Dreamers are motivated when they're invested in what they're working on.

Here are some choices you can give your kids:

- Amanda from Mexico lets her son do his homework with headphones because that's how he works best.
- Treasure from Hillsboro, Oregon, lets her kids decide where in the house they complete homework.
- I let my daughter turn our family room furniture into her personal desk because that's where she chooses to do homework.

Choices like these give kids control of their work environment, which ultimately makes them more productive.

Rewards also work very well with dreamers, as long as the reward is something that really interests them, which they can't get often or anywhere else. When my daughter started Kindergarten, I used those little Haribo packets of gummy bears for each homework session. Whenever she completed a page, she got a gummy bear, When she finished the entire assignment, I allowed her to eat the rest of the packet.

We'll get more into rewards in Part 2, where I'll also give you a list of potential prizes.

Whether you have a Quick Quitter, a Perfectionist, an Overwhelmed Kiddo or a Dreamer, it is possible to make homework drama-free in your home. Certain tactics will work better on each personality type and there will be some trial and error involved, but change is possible. Once you've nailed it, it's time to encourage certain behaviors and character traits that help make homework a breeze.

CHAPTER 6:

The Drama-Free Homework Ideal

One day, during flu season, my son stayed home sick from school. My daughter, ever the responsible older sister, offered to go to his classroom and pick up his homework for him. As she got home that afternoon, she invited him upstairs.

"C'mon buddy, lets go do our homework and watch *Kids Baking Championship*."

At first he agreed but then he slid into a gigantic meltdown.

"I DON'T WANT TO WATCH KIDS BAKING CHAMPIONSHIP! Sissy has the good lap desk and I have the broken one. MOM!! I can't draw a straight line without a RULER!"

I didn't fight him. I did take his homework packet away and suggest he try it again later, which ignited another meltdown. At the same exact time his sister trotted down the hall, announcing, "I finished my homework."

Of course.

Two hours later, when my daughter was at dance, my son sat down at the kitchen table and worked through his homework with focus and determination. Completely unprompted by me.

This is what we encourage through homework: the ability to focus, take responsibility and persist when at first it seems too hard.

It's the homework situation I hope for you in your own home. Is it perfect? No. But teaching children never lands in the world of perfection. Think more in terms of progress.

The following skills are what your elementary student is working on every time he or she sits down to work on home assignments. Don't forget: at elementary level these aren't just the skills needed to complete homework; developing these skills is the *purpose* of homework at this age.

Focus

Whenever I talk to a parent about homework drama, the number one complaint is always, "My child doesn't focus on her homework."

Treasure, a mom of seven, says, "All my kids drag out their homework time because they're messing around and playing in between. "

Kyda describes that her daughter, "gets very antsy, can't focus. I'm sitting next to her, constantly nagging her to get back to it or she gets frustrated with her math and just shuts down."

Focus is a huge issue. Even we adults struggle with it.

During homework, we expect kids to work on homework for a set chunk of time without becoming distracted. We want them to be able to self-regulate their attention and train their brains to work straight through.

Does this come easily? No. In fact, it takes kids many years to master the focus skill—many times it depends on the day. Approach this like working out a muscle at the gym. We practice so it gets stronger but we may never be able to deadlift 400 pounds. Lifting 200 pounds is mighty impressive, though, and should be celebrated.

Responsibility

It is not your responsibility that your child gets her homework done; it's hers and hers alone.

A friend of mine told me how, when her daughter threw tantrums during homework, she refused to sit and work with her any longer. In fact, she told her daughter that she wasn't in control of her emotions in that moment. My friend then signed her homework and wrote a note to the teacher saying that her daughter wouldn't complete it.

Your child refusing to do an assignment is not a reflection of your parenting. When you refuse to take responsibility for their homework, the responsibility automatically shifts to your child. She thinks, "If mom's not going to make me complete homework, then when it's not done, I'm the one who faces the consequences at school."

OK, let's be truthful: she'll think that eventually. When you first shift over to this tactic, she'll say, "But it's not my fault. You never reminded me."

Be prepared for that. Know that when you hear it, you're on the right track.

Other responsibilities that rest solely with the kids are:

- Keeping track of all homework supplies, and
- Deciding when to start and finish homework.

It is possible. Take Homework 911 students Celinda and her Kindergarten daughter, Celinda, She's part of a line of Celindas! How cool, right? I'm going to call the younger Celinda, C, to reduce confusion in this story.

Celinda was seriously at her wit's end when it came to homework. The homework packets that C's teacher sent home each week always caused a family fight. What made it extra hard was that Celinda works days and her husband works nights so C usually ended up doing her homework at the sitter's house.

And oh, there were so many fights. You know the feeling when you're trying to make a change in your child's behavior but the other people in your child's life aren't exactly on board? That's what happened here.

The sitter tried to get C to sit down and do homework, but she wasn't always successful. Celinda's husband also took a different approach to homework. He and C typically engaged in a battle of wills since he was unwilling to bend in any of his expectations for C's work.

All this over Kindergarten homework. Celinda called it "pure pain for everyone involved." Then, Celinda and C took Homework 911 and everything changed.

C took over. This strong-willed Kindergartener took responsibility for her work. She decided on the order to do things in the afternoon at her sitter's house. She designed what went into her homework box. C took charge.

What happened? There was no longer a need for Celinda to expect the sitter to enforce C's homework time because now C did it on her own. The fighting between Celinda and her husband decreased because now C told each parent **when** she would do her homework and **how** she was going to do it.

Celinda says the biggest breakthrough came when C realized, "it's really her choice. That it is up to her how, when, where, and with how much drama her homework gets done. This isn't something mommy and daddy are forcing on her. That it's her responsibility and life and she gets to choose."

Celinda says that C is now more independent and confident when it comes to homework. If this isn't happening with your child yet, don't worry. I'm painting a vision of the future for you. I'll guide you through setting up a homework routine that will teach your child how to be more responsible and eventually achieve this goal.

Time Management

Raise your hand if you struggle with time management. (My hand is raised high right now.)

There are tons of times I run late, leave a lot less time to do something than I need to get it done and watch Netflix when I'm supposed to be working.

But somehow, I manage to get the important stuff done. That's what time management is. It's not getting *everything* finished. Rather, its making decisions on what to prioritize and then getting things done....

...eventually. Doing it eventually. Getting it completed by the deadline.

If you grade yourself by this definition of time management, do you score high? I hope so.

That said, we all know how frustrating it is when we keep procrastinating on a task. Something that should take 20 minutes, ends up taking hours. We want to teach our kids how to manage their time early on, so homework doesn't do this to them.

And so homework doesn't take up all of family time, either.

Jennifer from Georgia uses a brilliant strategy to convince her boys to complete homework quickly: tablet time, which her kids really love. But she adds one extra layer to make the time management lesson stick.

Her boys are only allowed to use a tablet before dinner. In her house, dinner is at the set time of 5:30pm. She says they don't dawdle on their homework now because they know they will miss tablet time if they do.

Persistence

Success isn't based solely on talent. Rather, the most successful people are those who push through the failures and struggles, and never give up. Homework can teach our kids how to persist when they feel unmotivated or when it simply seems too hard to continue.

We want our kids to struggle. Just the other day, my daughter complained to me how she hated doing the Science Fair because, "something always goes wrong."

She continued, "Either we don't know how to do something, our experiment doesn't work or the paint on our display boards dries in splotches."

It took me a second because I was the kid who hated Science Fair, too, for these exact reasons. But now, after surviving not only science projects but my many failures in my adult career, I turn to her and say:

"Sweetie. I hate to break it to you but that's what life is like. Every failure is a learning experience and you just need to take it and keep going."

It's an impossible lesson for kids to learn if we shield them from the hard stuff. Or if we step in during Science Fair time and do it for them.

My dad once did a Science Fair project for me. During eighth grade, our science teacher assigned us a Rube Goldberg device which is a simple machine where one action sets off another action, and so on. After I sat there, stared and procrastinated until the weekend before, my dad took over. He decided what the machine would do: put a stamp on an envelope.

I begrudgingly worked along beside him as an assistant.

My project ended up being the best in the class. However, I didn't feel the victory.

Now, I don't want to place the blame on my dad here. Middle school grades were incredibly high-stakes for me as I was trying to qualify for a college prep high school. One bad grade could sink my application.

Why do we make life so high-stakes for 12-year-olds? When failure is so painful so young, we don't build kids' capacities to handle it in the future.

Here's what was reinforced for me during that Rube Goldberg project:

1. Rube Goldbergs are cool but completely inefficient. I mean, c'mon... just lick the stamp and put it on the envelope.
2. I'm not good at Science.
3. My dad had to do my project for me, therefore I'm not smart enough to figure this out.

I never attempted another science project in my entire life—at least, nothing that required real investigation or the possibility of being wrong.

In high school, I shied away from failure. I never developed a comfort with being slightly uncomfortable, and it's worked to my disadvantage more times than I can count.

That's not what I want for my kids.

(Dad: If you're reading this, this is not because of that one science experiment. I love you! You and mom did great with me.)

In elementary school homework, the high stakes are simply not there; now is the time to fail.

Now is the time to experiment.

Now is when kids can see that their failures don't end the world.

When kids are persistent, they know, "This is only *one* thing I've tried that didn't work. It's not me; I simply haven't found the right method yet."

They don't view failure as a judgement on their talent or ability. It's learning.

In her book, *Grit*, Angela Duckworth[9] defines the most successful people by how long they can persist with difficult tasks. Grit is defined as the ability to keep going, even when it's hard and uncomfortable. Grit keeps people practicing skills over and over again until they achieve mastery. It predicts a person's future success.

We want our kids to have grit.

We want them to know we can't "save them" when things get hard. Rather, we encourage and don't step in because we're confident they will figure it out themselves.

As long as their personal safety is not in danger, struggle will strengthen your child.

The trait of persistence also requires that kids know when imperfection is OK. Many kids become so cemented in a perfectionist mindset that they are never happy with their own work.

In her book, *Lean In*, Sheryl Sandberg[10] offers the maxim, "Done is better than perfect." We need our kids to work on a project and then push it out the door—especially if they struggle with perfectionism.

My son grapples with this now. One night, he sat at the kitchen table finishing his Kindergarten homework and started to cry. He slammed down his pencil with a grunt and yelled, "Ahhhhh, I'm no good at this!"

"What's going on buddy?"

"I can't get my letters to sit on the baseline!" he screamed.

Whoa. Ok, let's take a little step back. We all know the frustration about not being able to complete a task to our liking. Writing letters is a pretty low-stakes way to fail and experience that disappointment.

We stopped homework that night. I explained he was probably hungry or tired. He'd completed enough of his work so it was time to step away.

"But, no! I won't finish it."

I took the packet away and then sat down next to him. We cuddled as he broke down into sobs. Eventually, I convinced him to take a break and eat.

The next morning, before school, he erased those wayward letters and finished the rest in less than 5 minutes.

Persistence doesn't mean stupidly pushing through the point of frustration. At times, it means knowing when you're done - both mentally and with the task.

Done is Better Than Perfect.

Homework in elementary school is not about finishing "all the things" and doing them perfectly. Rather, it's your kid's low-stakes time to fail and practice the skills of focus, responsibility, time management and persistence. This time is about developing positive character traits, relationships and work habits.

But how do you develop them?

You need to teach your child a flexible homework routine.

What follows is the complete point-by-point plan to set up your drama-free homework routine and set your child up for success in later years.

PART 2:

Your Drama-Free Homework Plan

CHAPTER 7:

Setting the Homework Routine

This is it. Get ready to see your afternoons and evenings completely change.

Get this right and, instead of worrying about homework, your family will have less stress, less fighting and more time for the things you love to do.

Plus, you'll know you're setting your kids up for

success for their entire school career by nailing their homework routine now.

We've talked about appropriate homework, parent problems, the kinds of values and skills we're developing in our kids as well as how different personalities will respond to parts of this routine in different ways.

You're prepared. Now, let's put it into practice.

You're excited, right? I'm excited! First, let's address our potential stumbling blocks.

Routine Stoppers

No Motivation to Read

When I was a brand new teacher, I dreamt of changing the system, starting with inspiring a love of reading in my students. I loved reading - still do. I used to hide Babysitter Club books under my desk and read them so my fourth grade teacher, Mrs. Safford, couldn't see me (I have a feeling she knew exactly what I was doing and let it slide.)

As I planned the daily schedule for my fifth grade class, I left 20 minutes open for independent reading. I thought it was the dream: pick any book you want and read for 20 minutes. Basically, glorified free time backed by strong academic research.

Research says that the more you read, the more words you're exposed to and the better you get. It was a win in all ways.

Picture this: I'm a brand new, enthusiastic teacher bent on changing the world.

The first day of school, I took my students to the school library. They all brought back books and I set the timer for 20 minutes.

It was a complete and utter failure.

The first two minutes, the class was silent. But then Erick turned and started whispering to his friend. Jessica stared at the ceiling. Jeremiah got up from his desk because he broke his pencil.

What?!? You don't even need a pencil to read.

I didn't get it. I ended up cutting our independent reading time at eight minutes because only three out of 30 students were actually reading.

What gives? Some kids have not yet fallen for reading. And maybe they never will. Maybe they'll become die-hard fans of audiobooks; I don't know.

But what I do know is that the human brain is primed for a good story. We're all intoxicated by them. It's why I've littered little stories all throughout this book because—let's face it—a book containing just homework tips would be pretty dry.

You might be fighting with your kid about his or her

required reading time. He doesn't want to do it. "Books are boring," he says, as you bang your head repeatedly against the wall.

I argue that it's not books that are boring. It's that he hasn't yet found the right book.

There is no magic in liking to read. The power lies in the material.

If your student has not yet found the book that captures her imagination, it's time to experiment.

Start with her favorite movies and TV shows. You probably already know what she likes to watch. From there you can either do a quick internet search for similar books or talk to a local librarian who will be able to make excellent recommendations.

The Need to Move

Some kids need physical movement to focus. You've probably heard of classroom chairs that bounce or desks that kids can stand at: this is why. (Adults need this as well. My friend Brie tells me she needs to click on a pen to stay completely focused at work. She says it annoys other people, so she can't do it as often as she likes, but when she's alone its her secret to productivity.)

Some kids need to move before they can concentrate. If your child can't sit still at homework time, let her run around the backyard, dance in an indoor dance party or do a burpee. As everyone who has experienced burpees knows, they are the curse of every workout but guaranteed to tire out even the most energetic person.

Hangry

Before meeting my husband, I didn't believe Hangry was an actual condition.

However, oh my goodness! He displays the effects of hunger more visibly than anyone I know. He gets very quiet and answers me using only short responses: "Yes", "No".... that sort of thing. As soon as he gets food, his mood shifts 180 degrees.

My son is the exact same way.

If I try to broach a homework conversation when he's hungry, look out. He'll go full-scale screaming banshee right there on the tile floor of the kitchen.

Thus, snacks. Snacks are essential in our home. We have a shelf in our pantry dedicated to easy kid snacks. It holds items like:

- Goldfish crackers
- Peanut butter sandwich crackers
- Fruit cups with real juice
- Yogurt raisins
- Applesauce pouches

As you eye my list, you may think, "Wow, JoAnn, that's actually a lot of processed food with a fair amount of sugar."

Yes. Yes it is.

But, that's what my kids eat when they get home. Is it ideal? Nope. But it stops the Hangry before they get too out of control.

However, these snacks are never enough on their own. My son or daughter will grab one and then, when they're hungry again 10 minutes later—because that's the effect of processed food—their emotions have stabilized and they are much more amenable to taking a piece of fruit or a slice of turkey.

I ease in the healthy, sustainable food by letting them eat a bit of acceptable junk first. And it works—Hangry is under control in our house.

Another trick is to bring cold sliced apples with you when you pick kids up from school. Faced with the car ride home and nothing else to eat, most of the time my kids will take the apples and Hangry will be stopped before it has the chance to multiply.

Lack of Supplies

Picture this: your child walks in the door from school, sets down her backpack and takes out her homework.

Everything is going well.

Except… all of a sudden, her pencil breaks.

And while you purchased an entire pack of those Ticonderoga yellow pencils, now they are nowhere to be found.

There's no pencil in the kitchen drawer.

Nary a pencil in the backpack.

None in the cup on the counter.

To top it off, your electric pencil sharpener has suddenly decided to stop working. As you jam the pencil in, the sharpener responds with a soft *whir, whir*. What was once a good homework vibe comes to a crashing halt.

Yes, this happened to me.

My daughter started pacing back and forth across our kitchen floor. "What if we can't find a pencil? I'll get in trouble if I don't finish my homework!!"

I gritted my teeth. "We're going to find this pencil!"

Ten minutes later, I finally dug a sharpened pencil out of my glove compartment. What should have been a 20-minute homework assignment turned into 45 minutes… all because of *one* pencil.

There are moments where even your best intentions go flat.

I planned ahead; I got a pack of pencils. But at that moment, we mysteriously ran out (OK, if I'm honest, it wasn't so mysterious.)

When I was a classroom teacher, I quickly discovered that if I didn't have a procedure for every single action that took place in a classroom, my 30 students would soon erupt in chaos.

We had a hand signal for using the bathroom...

Sharpening a pencil...

Getting a drink of water...

Kids knew what to do when their pencil broke or if they forgot it at home.

I'm not saying that you go into quite this level of detail in your own home, but when it comes to homework, it helps to have a sacred place for homework supplies.

And by sacred, I mean that they are not touched, tampered with or even looked at unless it's homework time.

You need a homework box.

A homework box improved Anouk and her daughter Mia's homework routine. Anouk enrolled 8-year-old Mia in Homework 911 because she kept needing to remind her to focus. Mia would constantly get distracted and leave her homework to find a supply she needed.

The homework box took away the distraction of missing supplies meaning that Mia had more focused work time.

This is the first secret of a successful homework routine; let's look at them all.

Secrets of a Successful Homework Routine

Now that I've prepared you for what may go wrong and how to solve it, let's shift our focus to the things that work well.

Following are the secrets to a homework routine that rocks. Keep in mind that this is not a step-by-step process but rather a series of components. Every child is different; while some kids may need strict organization of their homework box to be successful, others will find that a schedule is way more important.

Try them all. Simple experimenting will soon tell you what works best for your kid.

All of these secrets are magic ingredients proven to build the skills of focus, persistence, time management and responsibility in a child.

Many of these secrets involve printables I've created to help you implement them. You can grab all the printables at **www.dramafreehomework.com**

Secret 1:

Rules of the Homework Box

Before we go over what's in your homework box, let's look at the rules.

If the term 'rules' is a little too harsh, you can call them procedures. But whatever you call them, don't skip this step.

Because you can pack a box with supplies and hand them to your kid, then all the supplies mysteriously disappear a week later. I know because I've done it. I wasted countless classroom dollars as a fifth grade teacher because I had no procedure for supplies.

When it came time for my own kids to start school, I knew we needed a process.

Enter the homework box.

At the beginning of the school year, I took my daughter and son to Target to pick out their own school supply box that would be kept at home in a drawer and store every item they needed to complete homework.

My daughter chose a pink case because, well... it's pink. And my son chose a green, bug-eyed monster case. Allowing kids to choose their own boxes helps create those feelings of ownership and responsibility over the box. It's theirs; they picked it, therefore they are more likely to take care of it.

Here's why the homework box works:

- It is **only** used for homework. Not for random art projects, a new house for Disney Princesses or a place to store LEGOs. Only homework.

Outside of homework time, I keep the box.

- Inside the lid is a checklist of all the supplies contained in the homework box.

After choosing the case, we stuff it with supplies. In our cases are:

- Colored pencils
- Scissors
- Pencil
- Glue stick
- Pencil sharpener

At the end of each homework session, my child is responsible for making sure that every supply comes back to the box. I affix a supply list with packing tape to the inside lid so that they can use a dry erase marker to take inventory before handing it back to me.

It may seem crazy checking the supplies in the homework box each day. But it's not forever.

If we checked to ensure our kids had all of their supplies everyday for eternity they would never learn personal responsibility nor experience the failure of losing a key item.

Rather, with the homework box, we are teaching our kids a homework organization habit that they can use for the rest of their lives.

The first week of school, yes, you will be checking the homework box every day. Depending on your child, you may be checking it for up to 6 weeks.

That's OK.

But once you see that they are returning all supplies to the box and checking each off the list, you can release a little control.

Secret 2:

Decide on the Order of the Routine

I've learned one major thing about picking my kids up after school. I cannot by any means ask them in any sort of cheery voice, "How was your day?"

My ten-year-old daughter recently told me that for some reason that question produces this fiery rage inside of her. I asked my husband about it that night and he said that the question has too many expectations attached to it. If someone really wants to know about your day, they will ask you directly with no fake cheer.

The cheer places too much of a burden on having to give a happy answer when in reality it might have been a disappointing day.

OK, I get it.

But then, I realize that the response to anything I ask my kids to do after school is met with groans and whines.

Why? Are your kids like this too?

After a long day of being told exactly what to do:

Where to sit...

How to talk...

The right way to hold a pencil...

I can see how more demands can push anyone over the edge. Especially when the person making those demands is Mom—the safest person to explode around.

This is where predefined expectations work really well. When we set a routine that kids know they're expected to follow each afternoon, we eliminate the whining and grumps.

We can simply point to our routine posted on the wall and not say a thing.

The trick is to:

- involve our kids in creating this routine; and
- write this routine down and post in a visible place near the homework area.

First, sit down and brainstorm together exactly what needs to be done after school. Do this step with your kids so they have ownership over the process.

Some ideas are:

- Unpack backpack.
- Take out homework folder and box.
- Do homework in kitchen/ office/ desk.
- Check homework with Mom/ Dad/ Grandma.
- Change out of school clothes.
- Get snack.
- Do homework.
- Make lunch for tomorrow.
- Count supplies in homework box and put backpack away.

You want to not only designate what you want done but also how you want it done. In other words, if your child needs to do homework, where should she do it? If he needs to have his homework checked, who should he check it with?

I created an after-school checklist that you can edit and make your own. You can download it here: **www.dramafreehomework.com**

Secret 3:

Take Out That Timer

Remember the last time you were overwhelmed? If you're like me, you'll probably be able to think of an example right away. I feel like I'm overwhelmed at least once an hour.

It's a problem. I'm working on it.

Usually, my overwhelm comes from thinking I need to do everything all at once. That big project I want to tackle? I see it fully, in all its steps, as one thing I need to do immediately, instead of breaking it apart and accomplishing one little chunk at a time.

Our kids get this way, too. My daughter participates in a team competition called *Battle of the Books*. Every quarter, each team reads the same four books and then competes head-to-head in Jeopardy-style questioning.

Without fail, she stresses at the beginning of each quarter, knowing that she needs to read all those books. Nevertheless, she pushes through and won't relent until she's finished them all.

However, some kids have the opposite response. Huge tasks shut them down.

It seems too hard; too long. They feel they'll never be done. So they sit and stare at their worksheet of 20 fraction addition problems. Or they freeze over their five-paragraph essay, barely able to write the first sentence.

Olivia, a Homework 911 mom from Arizona, describes the homework situation in her home as a never-ending event. It used to take her fifth grade daughter two hours to complete her homework each night.

Then, she introduced the timer.

Timers are wonderful tools because they define an end time. Instead of trying to motivate kids to write a paragraph that may take forever, it's easier to convince them to write for only two minutes.

Olivia was a little skeptical when she started with the timer. But the second day she told me, "I just walked into my bedroom to change and came back out to my 10-year-old already doing her homework, timer already set. Excuse me, what?! I've literally never seen this girl so self-motivated."

Timers work. They are so effective that I use them in my own writing. Whenever I sit down to write a blog post and all the voices come at me telling me how I can't write and I have no ideas left to share, I set my cell phone timer to 25 minutes. I tell myself, "Just 25 minutes and if I still feel the same way when the buzzer dings, I can move onto another project."

But usually I find my groove within that time span. Kids usually find their rhythm as well.

Timers are a way to stop all the self-defeating thoughts by giving your brain a set endpoint for work.

With your first adventure in timers, start with a very small chunk of time: 1-2 minutes. Their only goal is to work straight through the time block. That's it. Once the timer buzzes, hold a mini celebration. Maybe a run around the room or a stretch break. Then, set the timer and try it again. Work consistently until the timer rings.

Eventually, your child will either take ownership of the timer, like Olivia's daughter did, or won't need it.

I love my timer though. I wouldn't be as productive without it.

Secret 4:

Rewards

Oh, rewards! Many times you get a bad rap. Some people consider it bribery to use rewards... is this the route to independent homework? Surely not.

However, I've found rewards can be effective if:

- the rewards are short-lived.
- the child takes over the reward process.

95

The problem with any sort of reinforcement is that it can lose its effectiveness fast. Setting up a sticker chart or giving a treat at the end of homework ceases to become a reward after a while because kids adjust to receiving it. They start to expect the reward and it no longer serves as motivation for behavior.

However, rewards do provide the necessary motivation to kickstart a desired behavior, especially if your child is reluctant.

I told you at the beginning of this book how my daughter sat crying at our kitchen table every day after Kindergarten. She didn't want to even attempt homework, let alone finish it. I needed to give her a jumpstart.

Knowing that she loved gummy bears, I tore open a small package of Haribo and offered her one for each problem she finished. Her attitude immediately changed from complete refusal to, "Yes, I want a gummy bear."

The reward ignited her motivation.

The next day, I brought the gummy bears back. Except this time, she needed to do two problems for a gummy bear. We kept working this way for a couple of weeks until one afternoon she asked me, "Mommy, can I just do the whole homework packet and then I can have the whole packet of gummy bears?"

Sure. That's when I knew she formed a habit around doing her homework and no longer needed the frequent rewards.

I let that box of gummy bears run out and didn't buy any more. She no longer needed them for motivation,

For rewards, you can also use:

- fruit snacks.
- stickers.
- marbles in a jar.
- postponing bedtime by ten minutes.
- letting your child choose what the family eats for dinner.
- adding a minute to screen time.
- activity of choice after homework time.
- five minutes of your sole attention without any sibling interruptions.

Not all rewards work for every child. Choose a reward that you think will motivate and, if that doesn't work, experiment with something else.

Secret 5:

Tweak as necessary

The four main components of a successful homework routine are:

- making sure your child takes ownership of the routine by choosing when, how and where to work.
- ensuring basic needs like hunger and the need to move are addressed before starting.
- having all the necessary supplies to complete homework and asking your child to take charge of supplies.
- using motivational tools such as timers and rewards to encourage your kiddo to finish homework quickly.

Once you have these in place, you'll see a remarkable change in homework time.

Remember, this process is all about experimentation and finding the homework solution that works for your child. You will see massive success in some areas—for instance, you may find your child will do anything for a gummy bear. Other parts may not work as well. I know many kids who push back against a strict schedule and work better under loose guidelines.

Your goal is to do more of what works and lessen what doesn't. Think of yourself more as your child's homework consultant than the homework police. You're there to help her structure her homework time so she can find the way that allows her to be the most productive and happiest possible.

I do want to warn you that it's not going to be easy. There will still be tantrums, especially when adjusting to the change. However, I guarantee that over time you will see your child become more self-motivated. Even better, you'll find your own stress level decrease.

If at any time you need help in this process, I encourage you to check out my course for kids called *Homework 911*. In it, I guide kids step-by-step through setting up their own homework routine. You can find more info about it at **www.dramafreehomework.com.**

CHAPTER 8:

Your New Reality

M y daughter started her school homework journey
crying at the kitchen table. She's now in fifth grade
and I no longer oversee her homework.

Honestly, I didn't think I would get here! I wanted to
curse homework. To fight for my child not to do it.

When she sat crying, I blamed myself for pushing too
hard or maybe putting her in school too early.

But it's all OK. All kids need to struggle to grow. In our
case, she needed to master the homework overwhelm
to feel confident about tackling more complex tasks.

Homework is a huge opportunity for elementary school students to practice behaviors they need in the future, at a time when there are very few repercussions if they fail.

No, it shouldn't take two hours. With a solid homework routine, your kid can be in and out of nightly homework in less than 30 minutes. A little longer for fourth grade and up, but in no way should it monopolize the entire night.

Can you imagine? Your kid walks through your door and, without being reminded, starts his homework routine. All his school work is finished by the time you both agreed on.

No stress.

No tantrums.

No taking over your family's entire evening.

Welcome to your new reality of drama-free homework.

Acknowledgements

No one ever writes a book alone. This is my first one and I'm so incredibly grateful for the people who helped make it happen.

My husband, Josh. You're my best friend and my constant sounding board. Thank you for being a check against my constant "crazy," and supporting me when all I want to do is curl up and cry.

My kids, Camdyn and Erik. You're the reason, you're my 'why' and my constant inspiration for helping other families. I see you and want to help you in every way I possibly can.

My parents. You raised me to be independent and achieve at incredibly high levels. Mom, you sat with me and checked up on me during those horrendous weekly fourth-grade book reports. Dad, I hope I made you proud by bringing the benefits of homework front-and-center.

It's not just for memorizing useless material but for practicing executive functioning skills.

My little sister, Jamie, because I'm pretty sure you'd be mad at me if I didn't mention you in some way. I love you.

To my mastermind group. My gosh, you all keep me in check. I don't know where I would be in this business without you. Thank you Ruth for always telling me the truth and encouraging me to keep going. Thank you Tasha, Jennifer R, Saira, Jen D, Jennifer M, Laura, Abby, Shelley, Monica, Chrissy, Tess, and Melissa.

Thank you to my friends. You are always willing to listen, give advice and bring me back from going completely insane. Thank you Bridget, Brie, Jenna, and Shana.

A huge thanks to the No Guilt Mom tribe! Also, thank you to everyone willing to get on a video call with me to discuss the homework struggles in your own family. Those chats helped shape the content of this book so much! Thank you Michelle, Renee, Nicole B., Kendra, Celinda, Treasure, Kate, Jennifer, Nicole A., Amanda, Anna, Irene, Olivia and Kyda.

Thank you to my editor, Meg Ward. You were the first person to read this book and I so greatly appreciate your insight and suggestions. You made it infinitely better!

Thank you to Julia and the amazing baristas at Peixoto Coffee. I wrote this entire book in the mornings I sat in your shop. Thanks for always asking me if I need water, Kim, after I finished my coffee.

Last but not least, I would like to say a big thank you to the members of the Drama-Free Homework Book Launch Team. Because of you, this is getting out into the world. Thank you Amanda Harden, Ashley Bernal, Aysa Morgan, Bekah Morel, Beth Averill, Brandy Earls, Brandylyn Lemen, Caroline Smith, Catriona Crombie, Celinda Labrousse, Cheryl Borden, Colleen Wildenhaus, Christina Wellen, Crystal Kelliher, Denise Hamon, Devam Shah, Donna Vandiver, Elizabeth Lenz, Irene Segura, Iris Gutierrez, Jackie Beck, Janell Deal, J.E. Tagle, Jenna Taylor, Jennifer Scopel, Jouhaida Alrawi, Kami Lubinski, Kendra Riemermann, Kristi Slemko, Krystal Butherus, Latricia Jackson, Laurie Thomas, Lily Miu, Marcos Wagner, Meridith Todd, Monique Braun, Pam Isaacs, Rachel Jenkins, Rebecca Elwell, Rochele Porpora, Sarah Dew, Shana O'Mara, Tammy Boyce, Wendy Diaz, Yvonne Oliver, and Zochil "Zee" Eagan

Notes

1. Kelly Wallace, "Kids have three times too much homework, study finds; what's the cost?," CNN, August 12, 2015, https://edition.cnn.com/2015/08/12/health/homework-elementary-school-study/.

2. Evan Porter. "A second-grade teacher's unique homework policy once went viral. That should happen again," *Upworthy*, May 23, 2019, https://www.upworthy.com/a-second-grade-teacher-s-unique-homework-policy-once-went-viral-that-should-happen-again

3. Robert J. Marzano and Debra J. Pickering, "Special Topic: The Case For and Against Homework," Educational Leadership 64, no. 6, (March 2007): 74-79, http://www.ascd.org/publications/educational-leadership/mar07/vol64/num06/The-Case-For-and-Against-Homework.aspx

4. Tawnell D, Hobbs, "Down with Homework Say U.S.. School Districts," The Wall Street Journal, December 12, 2018, https://www.wsj.com/articles/no-homework-its-the-new-thing-in-u-s-schools-11544610600

5. Kate Thayer, "Should Kids Have Homework? The Great Debate," Chicago Tribune, August 9, 2018, https://www.chicagotribune.com/lifestyles/ct-life-homework-pros-cons-20180807-story.html

6. Robert J. Marzano and Debra J. Pickering, "Special Topic: The Case For and Against Homework," Educational Leadership 64, no. 6, (March 2007): 74-79, http://www.ascd.org/publications/educational-leadership/mar07/vol64/num06/The-Case-For-and-Against-Homework.aspx

7. Idit Katz, Avi Kaplan, and Tamara Buzukashvily, "The role of parents' motivation in students' autonomous motivation for doing homework," Learning and Individual Differences 21, no. 4 (August 2014): 376-386, https://doi.org/10.1016/j.lindif.2011.04.001.

8. Carol Dweck, *Mindset: The New Psychology of Success* (New York: Random House, 2006), 220.

9. Angela Duckworth, *Grit: The Power of Passion and Perseverance* (New York: Scribner, 2018)

10. Sheryl Sandberg, *Lean In: Women, Work, and the Will to Lead* (New York: Alfred A. Knopf, 2013), 125.

CPSIA information can be obtained
at www.ICGtesting.com
Printed in the USA
BVHW042158180919
558859BV00011B/161/P